This document is geared towards providing exact and reliable information in regards to the topic and issue covered. The publication is sold with the idea that the publisher is not required to render accounting, officially permitted, or otherwise, qualified services. If advice is necessary, legal or professional, a practiced individual in the profession should be ordered.

- From a Declaration of Principles which was accepted and approved equally by a Committee of the American Bar Association and a Committee of Publishers and Associations.

In no way is it legal to reproduce, duplicate, or transmit any part of this document in either electronic means or in printed format. Recording of this publication is strictly prohibited and any storage of this document is not allowed unless with written permission from the publisher. All rights reserved.

The information provided herein is stated to be truthful and consistent, in that any liability, in terms of inattention or otherwise, by any usage or abuse of any policies, processes, or directions contained within is the solitary and utter responsibility of the recipient reader. Under no circumstances will any legal responsibility or blame be held against the publisher for any reparation, damages, or monetary loss due to the information herein, either directly or indirectly.

Respective authors own all copyrights not held by the publisher.

The information herein is offered for informational purposes solely, and is universal as so. The presentation of the information is without contract or any type of guarantee assurance.

The trademarks that are used are without any consent, and the publication of the trademark is without permission or backing by the trademark owner. All trademarks and brands within this book are for clarifying purposes only and are the owned by the owners themselves, not affiliated with any others.

Table of Contents

Introduction

Imagine that you have just been given the assignment of reading a book with hundreds of pages. You have only two days to complete this task and produce a written report about the reading. Would you be able to accomplish this in a timely and effective manner?

The truth is, not many people are able to leverage such an accomplishment. In fact, it is assumed that only expert readers can do this, leaving the average reader struggling to get through even a few pages of a work at a time. To compensate for this, researchers have long debated that speed reading, or the ability to read rapidly by combining phrases and sentences all at once, is the key to acquiring vast amounts of information in a shorter period of time. It has also been suggested that this technique is able to improve reading comprehension when implemented effectively.

Today, you can find several online courses and applications that train individuals on speed reading. These courses aim to help readers improve their ability to comprehend materials without spending extensive time on the text. A strategy such as this one is truly effective for individuals that are required to read a great deal of material. Consider college students or graduate students. The work load is almost certain to be overwhelming; and professors are less inclined to sympathize with a student simply because she is required to read many books at a time. Instead, it is up to the student to develop methods and strategies that will enable him to move through the material much more quickly while still being able to grasp the information's content effectively. Thus, speed reading is a key element in producing these types of results.

This is not to say that this concept is widely accepted among all those who have studied this phenomenon. As you will learn in this book as well as throughout your continued study of speed reading, there are many researchers who believe that speed reading is ineffective in its ability to help a person retain information. For many experts, those who oppose speed reading are considered to be old-fashioned, myth-based researchers who have not fully understood the positive effects of speed reading. To these individuals — the ones that oppose speed reading — the reader can and will miss important details that are often grasped by those who take their time in reading a text. Theoretically, it would be impossible for a reader to comprehend the material effectively if time is not taken to focus or fixate on each word. This idea, however, could not be further from the truth. In fact, there is substantial evidence to validate that one's inability to speed read greatly hinders his progress in acquiring the information presented in a text.

Quintessentially, and for the sake of this book, we will explore the many benefits of speed reading, and will discuss various strategies that one can use to improve reading comprehension and completion.

Chapter 1 - What is Reading Speed and How Does It Work?

Reading speed or reading rate is best understood as the ability to engage all of your senses (hearing, seeing, thinking, comprehending) at a rate that is more effective and quicker than normal. By using your eyes, ears, mouth, and brain, you can employ the senses to increase the rate at which you read. Let's explore this in more details.

The first process in reading involves seeing the words on the page. For most readers, we are able to look at more than one word at time. In other words, we can read in clumps. Long ago, researchers believed that every reader read each word individually, which added to the amount of time it took to get through a book. But current research suggests that not only are we able to look at multiple words at once, but we are able to skip certain words while still acquiring a general understanding of the text. This all aids in our ability to speed read.

Because we are able to look at multiple words at a time, our ability to comprehend various terms is enhanced by our power to read quickly. Even if we do not know the exact meaning of every word, we can decipher its definition by using context clues. ("Context clues" are basically the words or phrases surrounding an unfamiliar term, which often provide a suggested meaning of the word.) For this reason, we can conclude that speed reading enhances reading comprehension. To understand this further, let's consider the following example.

For many non-native speakers, reading each individual word at a time can become tedious, especially when the words are unrecognizable. The majority of one's concentration is focused not on the meaning of the word, but whether or not it can be pronounced. This focus or fixation on each word takes away from one's ability to concentrate on the overall meaning of the text. Thus, we can deduce that those who read more slowly than others are lagging behind in their ability to comprehend a text. Therefore, by increasing one's ability to read, his concentration moves away from fixation and move towards the general meaning of the entire text. This is what makes speed reading a powerful and effective method for readers.

Consider another benefit of speed reading: enhancing one's memory. Believe it or not, being able to read at a faster rate challenges your brain to work harder at retaining the information given. This, in essence, strengthens the brain, which is like a muscle. The more practice or exercise you employ with speed reading, the more the brain is able to work more efficiently at locking onto the information that is presented.

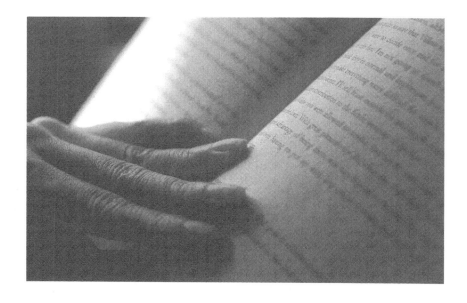

Speed reading is also a powerful concentration tool. Because one's reading rate is increased, the reader is required to maintain a sense of alertness as he reads. He must be cognizant of the author's main idea so as to retain comprehension effectively. Speed readers are sharp in their approaches because they understand that in order to get through a text in time, they must be more alert to details in the text that will enhance their understanding.

Thus, it can be concluded that increasing one's reading rate is essential to improving the quality and performance of reading, not to mention the ability to comprehend a text more accurately and effectively. As you move through the next portions of this book, you will learn about

different strategies and methods that will help
you improve your reading rates and reading
comprehension.

Chapter 2 - Strategies and Methods

Now that you have an understanding of what speed reading and reading comprehension are, it is now time to explore some of the strategies and methods that will assist you in increasing your reading rate. This section will address the following topics: meta-guiding, subvocalization, repeated reading, paired reading, easy extensive reading, and finally, skimming and scanning.

Chapter 2.1 - Meta-guiding

One technique that has helped individuals improve their reading speed and comprehension is meta-guiding. This method involves the use of a visual device — typically a finger, pen, or bookmark — that you use to guide your reading. Using this device will allow you to have control over your reading speed, and will assist you in focusing on the content more accurately.

To put this into practice, choose a book or reading text of your choice. Holding a pen or bookmark (or using your finger), drag the device along the lines of text. As you move along with it, you will realize that your ability to read through the text happens much more rapidly than without it. This is because your eyes work to keep up with the device. You will find that not only will you be able to move through the text more quickly, but your ability to comprehend the reading will also be enhanced because your eyes are not fixated on each and every word. Utilizing this technique is advantageous to the reader because it enables one to reduce the level of subvocalization, which often hinders a reader from moving through a text more efficiently.

To put this into practice, look at the following excerpt from the book, *The True Story of My Life: A Sketch*, by Hans Christian Anderson. To test your ability to speed read through this work, use a stopwatch and record the time it takes to read through the passage without employing a meta-guiding device. Now, after you have read it the first time, perform the same activity, this time using a device (writing utensil, finger, etc.). How long did it take you to read through the passage this time? Record the difference to determine whether or not you were able to implement this method successfully.

Excerpt from *The True Story of My Life: A Sketch* (translated By Mary Howitt, To Messrs. Munroe and Co) by Hans Christian Andersen:

> *My life is a lovely story, happy and full of incident. If, when I was a boy, and went forth into the world poor and friendless, a good fairy had met me and said, "Choose now thy own course through life, and the object for which thou wilt strive, and then, according to the development of thy mind, and as reason requires, I will guide and defend thee to its attainment," my fate could not, even then, have been directed more happily, more prudently, or better. The history of my life will say to the world what it says to me—There is a loving God, who directs all things for the best.*

My native land, Denmark, is a poetical land, full of popular traditions, old songs, and an eventful history, which has become bound up with that of Sweden and Norway. The Danish islands are possessed of beautiful beech woods, and corn and clover fields: they resemble gardens on a great scale. Upon one of these green islands, Funen, stands Odense, the place of my birth. Odense is called after the pagan god Odin, who, as tradition states, lived here: this place is the capital of the province, and lies twenty-two Danish miles from Copenhagen.

In the year 1805 there lived here, in a small mean room, a young married couple, who were extremely attached to each other; he was a shoemaker, scarcely twenty-two years old, a man of a richly gifted and truly poetical mind. His wife, a few years older than himself, was ignorant of life and of the world, but possessed a heart full of love. The young man had himself made his shoemaking bench, and the bedstead with which he began housekeeping; this *bedstead he had made out of the wooden frame which had borne only a short time before the coffin of the deceased Count Trampe, as he lay in state, and the remnants of the black cloth on the wood work kept the fact still in remembrance.*

Chapter 2.2 – Subvocalization

Subvocalization involves the process of internally "vocalizing" or hearing the words as you read them. This strategy is effective in terms of taking your time with the reading process; but it profoundly hinders the rate of reading. If you are looking to increase your speed reading, then one of the first steps is to eliminate subvocalization as much as possible.

To understand this concept in more detail, think of subvocalization as the internal voice that you "hear" when you read. Subconsciously, your listening and speaking skills are employed. This process was developed early on during the learning years of a reader. For example, when learning how to read, a person was instructed to read aloud. This strategy allowed the teacher to evaluate the effectiveness of the reader's fluency. By adapting to this technique, the reader subconsciously continued to "read aloud" internally as a way of engaging, comprehending, and determining the text's content. While this is a proven method for new learners, this also creates an obstacle for those who are trying to increase reading speed.

There are different methods that one can use in order to eliminate subvocalization. As long as the mouth is occupied with doing other things, this will enable the reader to avoid that voice that reads along with the text. Consider chewing gum, eating, singing, or anything that will help your mouth avoid the need to read aloud (internally or externally). Another effective strategy for eliminating subvocalization is to engage in repeated reading, generally of a text containing the same genre or jargon. In doing so, your mind is able to move swiftly across a work simply because it has become familiar with the terms, and has no need to vocalize each word in order to comprehend them.

The following excerpt will provide you with more practice in this area of eliminating subvocalization. For this activity, try a method such as humming while you read. Although there may be words that are unfamiliar to you, continue to peruse through the passage in order to assess how quickly you are able to read through it. As with the previous activity, record the time it takes for you to complete the reading.

As an added bonus, use a meta-guiding device to see if this further adds to your ability to increase your rate of reading.

The Secret Garden by Frances Hodgson Burnett:

When Mary Lennox was sent to Misselthwaite Manor to live with her uncle everybody said she was the most disagreeable-looking child ever seen. It was true, too. She had a little thin face and a little thin body, thin light hair and a sour expression. Her hair was yellow, and her face was yellow because she had been born in India and had always been ill in one way or another. Her father had held a position under the English Government and had always been busy and ill himself, and her mother had been a great beauty who cared only to go to parties and amuse herself with gay people. She had not wanted a little girl at all, and when Mary was born she handed her over to the care of an Ayah, who was made to understand that if she wished to please the Mem Sahib she must keep the child out of sight as much as possible. So when she was a sickly, fretful, ugly little baby she was kept out of the way, and when she became a sickly, fretful, toddling thing she was kept out of the way also. She never remembered seeing familiarly anything but the dark faces of her Ayah and the other native servants, and as they always obeyed her and gave her own way in everything, because the Mem Sahib would be angry if she was disturbed by her crying, by the time she was six years old she was as tyrannical and selfish a little pig as ever lived. The young English governess who came to teach her to read and write disliked her so much that she gave up her place in three months, and when other governesses came to try to fill it they always went away in a shorter time than the first one. So if Mary had not chosen to really want to know how to read books she would never have learned her letters at all.

Chapter 2.3 - Repeated Reading

For the purpose of informing the reader about the next following strategies, this and the subsequent sections will employ the expertise of Paul Nation (2009), author of the academic journal "Reading Faster." His study focused on how reading rates could be improved among school children, and he provided researched-based conclusions that highlight techniques used in order to increase reading fluency/comprehension as well as speed.

One of the first suggestions included the notion of repeated reading. As the term suggests, repeated reading involves the reader's ability to read a passage multiple times, especially complex passages. What happens to the mind is remarkable. For one, by re-reading an unfamiliar text, the reader is able to grasp the main idea of the work. Additionally, as she goes over the text again, her ability to read it more quickly becomes automatic simply because her mind has recognized the unfamiliar words as now familiar.

This is a tactic that is often used by educators to school-aged children. At times, the instructor will ask the students to read a text, let's say a poem. Because of the complexity of the work, the teacher will then instruct the students to read the passage again. At this point, the students should begin to develop a deeper understanding of the work because they have sifted through the complexity of the work. By reading the text even for a third time, the readers gain not only a better understanding of the passage, but they can also read through it more quickly than before. This is the power of repeated reading as it relates to reading rate and comprehension.

In this next activity, attempt to read the following text multiple times. On the first try, record the time it took to get through the passage. Read it again for a second time, also recording the time spent completing it. Read the passage again for a third time, and record the reading time. Do you notice any changes in the time it took to get through the passage? Are you able to comprehend the reading more effectively? Now, read the passage for a fourth round, this time employing the previous methods mentioned: meta-guiding and eliminating subvocalization. Can you see a difference in the time it takes for you to read through the passage as well as your ability to comprehend the text more adequately? If so, then you are already becoming seasoned in your ability to speed read. As you will find, the more you implement these strategies and methods, the more likely you are to have an increased reading rate.

Free from School by Rahul Alvares:

> *You must try to understand that when I finished school I was as raw as raw could be. I had never travelled anywhere on my own, never purchased a train ticket, since like most kids my*

age I had only travelled with my parents or relatives and they made all the decisions. I had no experience of how to handle money (my knowledge being limited to spending the 50 paise or one rupee I would receive as pocket money now and then).

So while I had set my sights on travelling far and wide my parents wisely thought that I should begin by learning to manage on my own within Goa itself. It was also the rainy season and travelling around the country would be much more difficult they explained.

So I started out by helping at an aquarium shop in Mapusa, the town nearest my village. The proprietor of the shop is Ashok D'Cruz, a college friend of my father's. I must tell you about Ashok. He is no ordinary businessman: keeping fish is a passion with him. He is far more interested in chatting with his customers about fish than making money selling them. I have never seen him forcing any of his *customers to buy from his stock of aquarium fish.*

In fact, it was Ashok who introduced me to the amazing world of aquarium fish way back when I was just nine and studying in Class V. Under his guidance then, I experimented with breeding guppies, platties and mollies, fairly simple types of fish to breed. However, it was a matter of great excitement for me at that time to be successful in my experiments and Ashok was generous enough to even buy back from me the baby fish I reared just to encourage me. Later I developed sufficient confidence to experiment with and breed more difficult types of fish, like Siamese Fighting Fish and Blue Guramies-all under the expert tutelage of Ashok.

Chapter 2.4 - Paired Reading

Because each individual has a different way of learning or mastering a technique, it is only fitting that there should be different ways in which one can enhance his reading rate. For many learners, paired reading is an excellent method of increasing reading accuracy, comprehension, and reading rate. This strategy involves the working of two individuals, one a proficient reader and the other a non-proficient. Each person is given a text to examine and read, and both are required to read it at the same time. For the sake of the non-proficient learner, the proficient reader reads at the same speed as the non-proficient. At times, the non-proficient learner can tap the proficient reader, indicating that she would like to read alone. Over time, the proficient reader will join again in the paired reading, especially if the non-proficient runs into problems with the text repeatedly.

The success of this technique is manifold. For one, any difficulties presented in the text are immediately addressed and corrected because the proficient reader will read correctly. For the non-proficient learner, this will instantaneously assist her in knowing what the accurate pronunciation of a word is, for example. Secondly, this activity works well for a proficient learner as he too is able to improve his reading rate.

For this next activity, try to find a person with which to partner. As with the other assignments, you will need a stopwatch or other timer in order to record the rate at which you both are able to read the text. Ideally, you will want to work with someone who is more proficient in reading than you are. This is not to embarrass or humiliate you, but rather to provide you with reading support. Remember, the purpose of this method is to help eliminate potential reading errors, especially because the proficient learner is already familiar with this type of vocabulary. Should you find yourself willing to read aloud on your own, feel free to tap the other reader. But keep in mind that if you happen to stumble upon words, the proficient reader will jump back in the activity. Once you both have gone through the passage once, record the time it took to complete it. As an added incentive to improving your reading speed, perform a second and even a third read of the following text, including reading with your partner. You may even want to use a meta-guiding device as a supplement to the activity. Once you have completed the following readings, analyze the difference in rates.

Old Greek Stories by James Baldwin

> *Perhaps no other stories have ever been told so often or listened to with so much pleasure as the classic tales of ancient Greece. For many ages they have been a source of delight to young people and old, to the ignorant and the learned, to all who love to hear about and contemplate things mysterious, beautiful, and grand. They have become so incorporated into our language and thought, and so interwoven with our*

literature, that we could not do away with them now if we would. They are a portion of our heritage from the distant past, and they form perhaps as important a part of our intellectual life as they did of that of the people among whom they originated.

That many of these tales should be read by children at an early age, no intelligent person will deny. Sufficient reason for this is to be found in the real pleasure that every child derives from their perusal: and in the preparation of this volume no other reason has been considered. I have here attempted to tell a few stories of Jupiter and his mighty company and of some of the old Greek heroes, simply as stories, *nothing more. I have carefully avoided every suggestion of interpretation. Attempts at analysis and explanation will always prove fatal to a child's appreciation and enjoyment of such stories. To inculcate the idea that these tales are merely descriptions of certain natural phenomena expressed in narrative and poetic form, is to deprive them of their highest charm; it is like turning precious gold into utilitarian iron: it is changing a delightful romance into a dull scientific treatise. The wise teacher will take heed not to be guilty of such an error.*

Chapter 2.5 - Easy Extensive Reading

Let's explore another technique called Easy Extensive Reading. Easy extensive reading is a method that many school-aged teachers use in order to assist their students in enhancing their reading proficiency. And while it is applicable to the classroom, it can certainly be used to help anyone who desires to increase his or her reading rate.

In its general sense, easy extensive reading requires the reader to take a text that is seemingly easy to read. In grade school, this would require, for example, a fifth-grader reading a third-grader's book. The idea is to work solely on the person's ability to read materials quickly. This, of course, requires that one is familiar with all of the words in a text. No difficulties should arise whatsoever simply because the reader is looking to improve reading speed rather than attempting to learn new information. If there is an unfamiliar word located in the text, the reader should be able to discern its meaning based on context clues.

Another form of easy extensive reading is to have a reader engage in books that are purely for enjoyment. Essentially, these books should also contain no difficulties that would prevent the reader from fully engaging with the text. Not only should these types of books be read, but they should be read often and in large quantities. In doing so, the reader is able to develop her reading fluency, which will inevitably lead to greater reading speed.

For this assignment, you will be asked to read an excerpt from *Alice in Wonderland*. This reading passage was chosen because generally speaking, people have some knowledge about this story. In summary, it tells the tale of a young girl who falls into a wonderland dream. The story is filled with adventure, suspense, and funny characters that keep the reader engaged. Several film makers have adapted this story, including Disney. For the most part, it is a book that one can thoroughly enjoy if he or she has a sense of imagination. Depending on one's reading level, this text may be simple or challenging to read. If it is simple, the rate of reading should be quick. If it is more difficult, then ideally one should employ the previous techniques and suggestions presented in the other sections. This can include meta-guiding, repeated reading, and paired reading.

As you read through this passage, take note of how well you are able to flow through the text because of your familiarity with most if not all the words. You will want to record your time as well. Because this book is fictional and contains a great deal of imagery, it will be advantageous for the reader to partake in other texts with similar themes of imagination. This type of entertainment will surely add to one's ability to read more quickly. In addition, books such as these will sharpen one's ability to comprehend materials more efficiently and adequately.

Alice in Wonderland by Lewis Carroll (Charles L. Dodgson):

Alice was beginning to get very tired of sitting by her sister on the bank, and of having nothing to do: once or twice she had peeped into the book her sister was reading, but it had no pictures or conversations in it, "and what is the use of a book," thought Alice, "without pictures or conversations?"

So she was considering, in her own mind (as well as she could, for the hot day made her feel very sleepy and stupid), whether the pleasure of making a daisy-chain would be worth the trouble of getting up and picking the daisies, when suddenly a White Rabbit with pink eyes ran close by her.

There was nothing so very remarkable in that; nor did Alice think it so very much out of the way to hear the Rabbit say to itself, "Oh dear! Oh dear! I shall be too late!" (when she thought it over afterward, it occurred to her that she ought to have wondered at this, but at the time it all seemed quite natural); but, when the Rabbit actually took a watch out of its waistcoat pocket, *and looked at it, and then hurried on, Alice started to her feet, for it flashed across her mind that she had never before seen a rabbit with either a waistcoat pocket, or a watch to take out of it, and, burning with curiosity, she ran across the field after it, and was just in time to see it pop down a large rabbit hole under the hedge.*

Chapter 2.6 - Skimming and Scanning

Let's explore a final strategy that is also sure to improve reading speed and comprehension: skimming and scanning. By definition, skimming is to go through a text quickly, generally looking at the surface of the work to identify what actually needs to be read in greater detail. This is beneficial to the reader because she can look at a book beforehand by skimming it to determine whether or not it is something that would interest her. In other cases, skimming is vital to those who have to read through a great deal of content. Rather than reading word-for-word, a person can skim through the materials to accurately identify the information that is most needed.

Scanning, while similar to skimming, involves the deliberate attempt to look for specific information in a text. For example, you may be asked to find information about a certain person, a date, or event. Rather than reading a book from cover to cover to find that information, you can scan the text. This particular strategy is not entirely effective in enhancing one's comprehension of the text. Nevertheless, it is a vital method in sharpening one's skills at reading through a text more quickly. Those who are able to exercise these strategies will find that reading large quantities of information is doable and practical. Furthermore, they will see just how effective they can be in acquiring information within a shorter period of time.

Like the previous reading passages, this excerpt from *A Christmas Carol* is one of pure enjoyment. It is the story of a grumpy, old man who must learn the importance and value of Christmas. After being haunted by three spirits, the protagonist, Ebenezzar Scrooge, develops a kinder heart, and determines to live his life as one who is thankful for the many blessings he possesses. Stories like these are truly effective in helping individuals improve their reading rates as well as their comprehension skills.

Generally, when skimming and scanning through a text, you are looking for surface-level information, or facts that can be quickly located. In theory, this should not take you much time because you are eliminating subvocalization and focusing your attention on finding the correct information. Without realizing it, you will find yourself understanding portions of the text without having to read every single word. In fact, the more you are able to perfect this skill, the stronger your abilities will be in terms of increasing your reading rate.

In this activity, rather than reading the passage thoroughly, skim and scan through it to find important information. In order to accomplish this, find the answers to the following questions using as little time as possible. You can use this same technique with a reading partner. For example, you both can have questions prepared for a specified passage. You can time each other to see who can find the answers more quickly. In doing so, you both create a healthy, educational challenge that will inevitably sharpen your skills to read quickly.

1. What was Scrooge's partner's name?

2. What happened to Scrooge's partner?

3. Were Scrooge and his partner friends?

A Christmas Carol by Charles Dickens:

> *Marley was dead: to begin with. There is no doubt whatever about that. The register of his burial was signed by the clergyman, the clerk, the undertaker, and the chief mourner. Scrooge signed it. And Scrooge's name was good upon 'Change, for anything he chose to put his hand to.*

Old Marley was as dead as a door-nail.

Mind! I don't mean to say that I know, of my own knowledge, what there is particularly dead about a door-nail. I might have been inclined, myself, to regard a coffin-nail as the deadest piece of ironmongery in the trade. But the wisdom of our ancestors is in the simile; and my unhallowed hands shall not disturb it, or the Country's done for. You will therefore permit me to repeat, emphatically, that Marley was as dead as a door-nail.

Scrooge knew he was dead? Of course he did. How could it be otherwise? Scrooge and he were partners for I don't know how many years. Scrooge was his sole executor, his sole administrator, his sole assign, his sole residuary legatee, his sole friend, and sole mourner. And even Scrooge was not so dreadfully cut up by the sad event, but that he was an excellent man of business on the very day of the funeral, and solemnised it with an undoubted bargain. The mention of Marley's funeral brings me back to the point I started from. There is no doubt that Marley was dead. This must be distinctly understood, or nothing wonderful can come of the story I am going to relate. If we were not perfectly convinced that Hamlet's Father died before the play began, there would be nothing more remarkable in his taking a stroll at night, in an easterly wind, upon his own ramparts, than there would be in any other middle-aged gentleman rashly turning out after dark in a breezy spot -- say Saint Paul's Churchyard for instance -- literally to astonish his son's weak mind.

Conclusion

By now, you should have a better understanding of speed reading and the role it plays in enhancing one's reading comprehension. Being able to increase the rate of reading is a skill that many proficient learners have acquired, and it is definitely something that can be learned for non-proficient readers and learners. The key to mastering this technique, however, is to continue practicing your reading on a regular basis. You will find that with time, patience, dedication, and determination, the rate at which you read will increase dramatically. Not only that, you will be able to comprehend the material more effectively because your fixation will not be on individual words but rather the general message of the text. Developing your ability to speed read is advantageous in many spheres, so it is vital that one cultivates this capability immediately.

If you are looking to increase your reading rate, consider the strategies and methods that were discussed in this book. Remember to eliminate what is called subvocalization, or the internal voice that is used when attempting to read each individual word. Instead, work to curtail this habit by reading large portions of words at the same time. Not only will your reading rate increase, but your ability to comprehend the overall text will be enhanced. Other methods that one can employ are reading texts repeatedly over a period of time. This is especially helpful when confronting difficult material or readings that contain unfamiliar content and vocabulary. By going over the information more than once, you begin to move through the difficulty, thereby increasing your reading rate as well as your comprehension. Reading alongside another reader, preferably one who is more proficient than you are, can also aid in your ability to speed read and comprehend. Remember that by pairing with an expert reader, you can learn how to pronounce uncommon words more accurately. And lastly, consider how effectively you increase your comprehension and reading speed skills when you employ the Easy Extensive Reading strategy as well as Skimming and Scanning. With these, you can practice increasing the rate at which you read remarkably. Above all else, practice, practice and practice! No one ever perfected a skill by completing a task once. By employing these strategies as often as possible, you are certain to improve your reading skills, thereby becoming a proficient learner.